You Are Your Soulmate

Choosing to Love and Accept all Parts of Yourself

Becky Kronske

Becky Kronske LCPC CCHt

618 W Griffin Dr Suite L

Bozeman, Montana 59715

(406)600-0763

www.beckykronske.com

ISBN: 978-1-7357601-0-0

Cover design by Nirkri fiverr.com

Edited by Tamelynda Lux

First Printing: December 2020

About the Author

Becky Kronske is a licensed mental health professional and a certified clinical hypnotherapist through the Hypnotherapist Union Local 472. She has over 15 years of experience in mental health. She is also certified in Reiki and Rapid Transformational Therapy. She runs a successful private practice in Bozeman, Montana.

Why Read This Book

Do you often find yourself in anxiety and worry? Are you often worried about what might happen or what others might think? Are you like so many others and attempting to control what is outside of you to avoid suffering? You may not understand that it's not the outside that is the threat, but how you end up treating yourself that creates the suffering.

This book explains why the relationship we have with ourselves is so important and is directly related to how we experience our reality. It is not what is happening that is the problem but our perception of it. You will get tools and knowledge to help you create the best relationship with yourself possible. Which, in turn, will provide massive emotional shifts in your life, creating peace, calm, and joy. You may be able to walk away from all the toxic people in your life, but you can't walk away from yourself. The good news is that you can change yourself, how you treat yourself, how you see yourself. Don't wait a moment longer to start the best relationship of your life.

Table of Contents

Chapter One

Your Relationship

What if the relationship you have with yourself directly reflected the state of the world? What if how you felt about yourself, how you viewed your worth, how well you forgave your mistakes, and how you spoke to yourself directly affected how you saw and experienced the world? If you considered yourself as worthless, unloving, not good enough, those would be the lenses through which you perceive the world. "But I am much kinder to others than I am myself," you might say. What if that didn't matter? What if your happiness in life has everything to do with your relationship with yourself? Would you be motivated to change? If that hasn't inspired you, consider this: Why would you want to spend a day out with someone that constantly puts you down? What would motivate you to have the best relationship you can? You have committed to spend eternity with yourself. What kind of relationship do you want with you? The relationship you have with yourself is the most important relationship you will ever have.

You are your soulmate. What does that mean? Permit me to tell you a bit about me first and why I felt compelled to write this book, and that might start to answer that question. Today I am a licensed mental health therapist. I have been in working in the mental health field since 2005 when I started working in a group home for boys. I have worked with children, teens, and adults. For many years I worked in crisis management to prevent suicide. I am obsessed with learning and continue to study, constantly reading and taking courses. As a certified clinical hypnotherapist, I am certified in stress management. I studied Reiki, and at the time of writing this book, I am working to be certified in brain health coaching. My obsession has been to figure out why we suffer so deeply and how to find a way out of that. How do we find peace and happiness? What I found is that our relationship with ourselves plays a huge role in this. How we talk to ourselves, what we think of ourselves, what we want from ourselves, how we handle failure all reflect how we perceive and experience the world. I decided to write this book because I wanted to share the tools and knowledge I have learned that helped change my life. In this book, I will help you understand how and why you are your soulmate. I will give you the techniques I use with myself and my clients to take any relationship you currently have with yourself and make it better. If you currently have a horrible relationship with yourself, this book is for you. If you have a wonderful relationship with yourself, this book can still help and make it even better. If you are unsure of what kind of relationship you currently have with yourself, this book will also help. We are all in different places in our lives, but what most of us have in common is searching for feeling the best we can.

I am no stranger to being my own worse enemy. By the time I was an adolescent, I had mastered the technique of self-hate, and no one could be crueler to me than I was. I was miserable and had no idea how to get out. Along came college and a course in psychology, which was so intriguing to me. It offered some explanation as to why I felt the way I did. It wasn't until my early twenties that I realized I was tired of hating myself. It was EXHAUSTING! It takes way more energy to hate oneself and resist all one's unpleasant emotions than it does to love and accept oneself. That day I made a choice. I decided I would figure out what in the world this *self-love* thing was all about.

What I have discovered is how to wake up and take responsibility for my life, which, in my opinion, has value beyond any monetary investment. Many people would disagree and do not want to accept this. I won't lie and tell you it's easy. Les Brown, a motivational speaker whom I admire and has an inspiring story, often says in his talks, "You do what's easy, life will be hard. You do what's hard, and life will be easy." I have found no truer words. Taking responsibility for your life is hard because we all have done and said things of which we are not proud. We have all had something done or said to us, which hurt immensely, and no one apologized for or acknowledged our pain and suffering. It is hard to take responsibility when it seems those around us aren't doing the same and just want to blame us. Pride can be a nasty, powerful entity. But all this brings is fighting, fighting others, and fighting ourselves. It can feel so completely hopeless and helpless, feelings of which I am not a fan, but freedom comes in embracing all emotions. Freedom comes when you quit fighting reality, judging it as wrong because it's not what you want it to be.

Freedom comes when you take responsibility for where you are and start looking at how your thoughts and actions got you where you are, without blaming others. Yes, people participated, but you participated, too, even if that participation was masked in good intentions. I promise you – you are the creator of your reality. As long as you refuse to accept or believe this, you will feel like a victim, and the world will be happening *to* you, not *with* you. Once you accept and take responsibility that your choices have brought you to where you are today, you can finally put yourself in a position to create change. The relationship with yourself is a direct reflection of your experience with reality. When you have a poor relationship, that is the lens you will be looking through, giving back a poor reflection, and a positive, loving relationship gives a positive, loving reflection. The choice is always yours. You are free to experience life in whatever way you want, through whichever lens you choose. Will you be the victim or the hero of your story? I have already played the victim, and I did not enjoy the role. Today I am the hero of my story, and I hope you choose to put on your hero's cloak too. You do this by choosing to love and accept all parts of yourself, light and dark. Self-acceptance can be one of the hardest things to do, but it is also one of the keys to happiness. To love ourselves, we need to accept everything about ourselves: that which we enjoy and brings us joy and that which brings us sadness, anger, or anxiety. You are already perfect in every way. As I tell my clients, your job is to ***heal*** until you realize that there was nothing wrong with you to start with.

You can always go back to the way you were. It is not wrong or bad to hate yourself. It also isn't pleasant, which is the main reason to continue with your journey in creating the best relationship with yourself. If you keep doing the same things you have always done, you will keep getting the same results. This includes your thoughts. If you keep thinking and focusing on the same beliefs you have held, you will keep receiving the same experiences. Does change feel risky? Probably. The brain tends not to like the unfamiliar and will pressure you to stay with what is familiar even if it is miserable. What I am offering, though, is knowledge, tools, and a chance to experience life from a different perspective. It is not really what happens to us that is the problem; it is how we perceive what is happening to us. Allow me to help you change that perception. Keep reading and allow me to show you how to have a relationship with yourself that is whole, happy, and healthy.

The world today is filled with people who have horrible relationships with themselves. So awful, they spend most of their money and effort trying to get away from themselves through alcohol, drugs, television, food, gambling, shopping, and more. Many people are in a state of survival. It is so miserable being alone that all they can focus on is doing whatever they can to keep their head above water. If something or someone comes along and triggers one of their pain centers, watch out – enter fight or flight response. That has been my experience, and I am willing to bet that it has also been your experience because you have picked up this book. Let me share a very general example.

You have a child that is born to two seemingly steady, healthy parents. The child is raised in a home that encourages politeness, obtaining good grades, respecting others, and listening to adults. All of these things sound good. Yet as this child grows up, this child feels sad. They are unhappy with their life and is unsure why. Maybe this child attempts to express this to their parents. They tell the child they have no reason to be unhappy. They have a good home, parents who are together, food on the table. The child begins to feel guilt for being ungrateful and slowly becomes angry with themselves, attempting to suppress the hurt feelings. The child doesn't want others to see how ungrateful they feel and focuses more on others and helping them because maybe this will help them feel like a *good* person. Yet, if those this child helps are not appreciative, the child becomes anxious and angry. They begin blaming others for being selfish and start pushing people away. Now we have an adult who feels lonely and struggles to connect to others. This adult spends a great deal of time, avoiding paying attention to their feelings by eating, binge-watching television, or working. Being alone is something this lonely, struggling adult dislikes and is not sure why, but knows they feel anxiety and sadness when alone.

Does any of this sound familiar to you, even vaguely? Maybe it is not being alone you dislike, but you feel anxiety when around others, or perhaps you think you are a decent person but cannot seem to get ahead in life. Possibly you feel like the world is out to get you, and no matter what you do, nothing seems to work, leaving you feeling lost, confused, or angry. A poor relationship with ourselves can manifest in so many ways. All of them are unpleasant, and yet it doesn't have to be this way. Often people believe that what is happening outside of them is creating suffering and distress. It can convincingly seem that way with financial woes, fights with loved ones, or loss. It is not what is happening outside of yourself that is the big issue; it is how you end up treating yourself internally, which creates suffering and distress. That is good news because if you had to change everything outside of you to feel good, you might imagine that it would take a while. Even though loss and stress are real, it is how we handle it internally that is the underlying problem. How you treat yourself when you perceive things not going as wanted is also the problem. This, too, is good news because you have control of that! There is only one person you need to change – you – not the world. Sounds good, right?

Take our earlier example of the adult who feels lonely and struggling. After many years of suffering and feeling lost in life, one day, they realize that they are tired of shaming and attaching guilt to themself. They are tired of putting themselves down every time something doesn't go as they think it should have. This adult has been calling themselves names, like dumb and stupid, and became tired of that, too. They have been doing this for most of their adult life, achieving feelings of anguish, pain, and misery. Basically, the relationship with themselves is a very poor one. So, they make a choice. It is as simple as that. But it is not a choice they make once. It is a choice they make over and over again – every day, in every moment. It is a bit like the idea of marriage. When two people take vows to love and support each other, those vows are not just for the wedding day. Those vows are to be honored every day the couple is together, including through the easy times and the hard. When you decide to change the relationship with yourself, it is a simple choice that must be made over and over. Seems like too much work? You don't need to change. You are free to keep your internal voices and beliefs just as they are, but I ask you: How is that working for you? Are you ready for a change? If you want things to be different, then *you* need to be different. As Albert Einstein said, "The definition of insanity is doing the same thing over and over expecting different results." What I am going to do is give you some knowledge about yourself and how your brain works, then powerful tools on how to create an amazing relationship with yourself. You will understand and appreciate how to be your soulmate.

What if life could feel peaceful? What if you enjoyed your own company? What if doing this work created a life in which you found joy, fun, and friendship? What if you discovered how to love yourself? What if, what if, what if? Here is what I want you to do. Take a few deep breaths and center yourself. Imagine you are way in the future, much older than you are now. You are looking back at your life and the choices you have made. What do you think you would regret more? Playing it safe and living a life with little change, or taking a risk, giving it your all, even if you mess up? Do you want to live a life of what-ifs?

Those who are close to death don't tend to regret the things they did, but they regret the things they didn't do. When you make the same choices and keep the same beliefs, you close the door to possibility, or at least it shrinking tiny. I am offering you an opportunity to change, first, by helping you gain some knowledge about the power of your brain and then how to harness that power. I will also give you tools that will help you to have a better relationship with yourself. Together we will go into the past and work with your inner child addressing the parts of you that were hurt long ago and still feel hurt today. By the end of this book, you will have learned how to see yourself compassionately. You will have learned how to have a better relationship with yourself, which in turn will improve your relationship with the world outside of you. When you venture into the unknown, you open that door wide to options and new possibilities. It can be both scary and exciting and very worth it.

Many of my clients have found this knowledge and tools you are about to explore to be life-altering. The rest of this book will help you understand the power of imagination and who you indeed are. This book will open the door to creating a relationship with yourself that you may have never thought possible. When you change the relationship with yourself, the relationship with others will change as well. When your relationship is based on respect, forgiveness, acceptance, and compassion, not only is your life filled with so much more peace, but you will find those attributes in others around you as well. Nothing feels more trapping than thinking you need *things* or *approval from outside of you* to feel better. When you learn how to give validation and receive acceptance from yourself, you are free from needing it from others. Not only am I offering a better relationship with yourself but also a feeling of freedom. It is almost like getting rid of debt. Instead of putting your money (energy) into your debt (needs from outside of yourself), you will be free of debt and, therefore, much more abundant in energy and strength.

Chapter Two

What Does Love Have To Do With It?

What is love? You search the world wide web, and you will find that love is generally defined as having a great interest or pleasure in something, but I think there is so much more to love than that. What can get confusing is how to love yourself and another at the same time. This was a lesson I learned many years ago through one of my jobs. I believed that love could conquer all. While working with crisis and suicide, there was an individual with whom I often worked who was verbally abusive. Like so many others I had worked with, this individual had experienced trauma as a child. The first few years of their life were with an inconsistent, abusive, and neglectful parent. As a child, they were removed from the home and adopted by another family.

Those first few years of development in a child's life are very important. Unfortunately, this young child had acquired post-traumatic stress disorder (PTSD), attachment disorder, and a feeling of danger and distrust of others. This led to acting out from childhood into adulthood; however, their behavior was not who they were deep within. This individual was also very caring, creative, funny and I often enjoyed our conversations. I thought if I could show this individual patience and understanding, they would be able to begin to see themselves through my eyes. It seemed to make so much sense. But that's not what happened. They also continued to be verbally abusive. I was confused as to why they could not see my care for them. The client continued to see me as someone unsafe and hurtful to them. I was thrown for a loop as my belief that love could conquer all was clearly being challenged, and I had to admit that I might have been wrong about love conquering all. That is when I realized that in this situation, I did not love myself. Instead, I was telling myself that it was loving not to take this person's behavior personally because it wasn't and that I should have patience and understanding. I thought for sure that I was creating a *loving* situation and holding space for them. What I didn't do was include myself in that equation. I didn't see how unloving it was for me to tolerate the verbal abuse. Once I saw how I was not loving myself in this situation and how I was approaching it, I was able to see I actually wasn't creating a loving situation for the client either; I was enabling the abusive behavior. Tolerating how this person lashed out and making excuses for their behavior was rewarding negative behavior and therefore enabling this individual to remain in a verbally abusive pattern. Their pattern was to lash out, and by not setting a boundary, I joined in with their pattern. We are all responsible for ourselves, and even if I had set boundaries initially, this individual could still choose to repeat their behavior, but I would at least not be a participant. I believe we are all good inside. So, by allowing this individual to abuse me verbally, I also think I was allowing them to abuse themself. My perception about this person was that they were struggling to forgive themselves for the cruel things they had said. Every time they were cruel to me, it confirmed their belief that they were worthless, leaving them feeling empty and unhappy, having no idea how to heal, looking to others to fill that need to feel better. They knew I wanted for them what they wanted for themselves, which was to feel happy and enjoy life. This person was always regretful after lashing out, whether it was to me or someone else. It was something they did not like about themselves, and their dislike and shame of it created more internal pain. They did not see how they could be happy with life and enjoy it when they could be so cruel to others. Are you beginning to see the pattern here? This individual believed they were worthless and unlovable, leaving them feeling emotionally miserable. They looked to others to find solace, and anytime they felt threatened, they lashed out, confirming their belief of worthlessness and unlovability, and again looking to others for solace.

Perhaps talking about loving yourself or even another creates discomfort in your body. It might feel stupid or silly. But I think the problem we see in this world is due to so many people not knowing how to love themselves, and even worse, we are often taught that loving ourselves is bad. Many of us were raised to share our toys with others, coached to *be nice to Timmy or Sally,* and not to be selfish. We learned that being selfish is wrong, and that makes you a bad person. If you take a step back and observe the people in your life, you will see many of them are working hard to prove they are a *good person.* They give up on their needs to give to others. We have been told this is loving. The main reason we are willing to fall into this pattern is that we want to be loved. We come to believe if we give of ourselves and are selfless, then we will be loved, except it doesn't usually work out that way. So why not? Why does it seem when we put out love, we don't always get it back? It may be because the more profound belief and reason you are so willing to give of yourself is that you don't love yourself enough. Now there is the other end of the spectrum, in which this individual mentioned earlier would fall. There are those that seem to take from others endlessly. It comes from the same issue. They don't know how to love themselves, so they are looking to others to fill that, but since they don't believe it themselves, it is like trying to fill an endless pit. Whether you are the one who gives or the one who takes, you will find yourself limited in your happiness until you learn to give to yourself. I am all for a world of giving to others, and what is best for others can also be what is best for you. First, let's have you understand how to find what is best for you.

Perhaps you have heard the saying that you need to fill your own cup first. Let's look at that idea on a spectrum. On one end of the spectrum, you don't believe you are lovable. You give to others because it feels good to do so. You think giving to others makes you a good person and so you keep giving to prove you are a good person. The problem that comes up is when your giving is not accepted or appreciated. When you give, and the other person denies it, it is much harder to convince yourself that you are a good person. Sure, you can put the other person down to help convince yourself. They are rude, selfish, undeserving, and so on. But when that happens, you have to ask yourself, am I really giving just to give, or am I giving so I feel good and loveable?

What about the other end of the spectrum? This is where your cup is already full of feeling worthy and lovable. It is so full it is overflowing, and you want to share that joy. Misery may love company, but so does joy. The difference is since your cup is full, you don't actually need anything from the other person. They could turn down your giving, and it wouldn't bother you as your cup is overflowing with good feelings. You are not looking to the other to fill your cup with their appreciation or gratitude. Sure, you may want them to feel as good as you, but you don't *need* them to feel as good as you. Do you see the difference? In the first example, when you give, you are looking for something in return to help you feel better. In the second example, you already feel better, and you don't need anything in return; you just want to share because that feels good in and of itself.

We are social creatures, and connections with others are deeply important to our survival. Babies will die if they are not provided touch and love, even if they are fed. I believe that we can help each other heal, but we must first start with ourselves. The relationship with yourself will directly affect your relationship with the world. I am going to teach you how to begin to fill your own cup. Maybe you are someone who dislikes yourself. Perhaps you tell yourself that you are worthless and don't deserve love. So, let me ask you, is a newborn baby worthy? Does that baby have to do anything to earn worth? On the assumption that you have said no, consider at what point does a baby need to start earning its worth? And who gets to decide its value? The parents? What if that child has abusive parents? What if one parent says that child is worthy, but the other doesn't? Which parent is right? At no point do we need to start earning our worth. It is something with which we are born. It is our inherent right. What often confuses people here is the perception that those who hurt others are worthless. It can be a difficult one to wrap your mind around, but those who hurt others still have the same amount of worth. It is actually their belief of worthlessness that can cause them to hurt others. Going deeper into why this is beyond the scope of this book, but this comes back to my point that learning how to love ourselves is needed in this world. When we learn how to fill our own cup, the chances of harming others drop drastically. Instead of living in a world where we position ourselves as needing something from someone else so we can feel better, and we become strong in soothing our own needs, we become less dependent on the responses of others. Again, this does not mean we approve of abusive or harmful behaviors.

The situation with a client may help to explain this. I spoke one day with my client, and she became upset with something I said when needing to end our session soon. She began to call me a worthless therapist and several other harsh names and threatened to tell my supervisor how awful I was. She did not want to stop talking and be alone. She lashed out because her fear of being alone was so intense, she did whatever she could to avoid it, including verbal abuse and threats. I understood this clearly and knew it had nothing to do with me and all to do with her past trauma. If I was to include myself in that equation of creating a loving situation, what would that mean? It would mean I would have had to acknowledge that it hurt me when the client was verbally abusive towards me. Acknowledging love for myself first means removing myself from a harmful situation. When the client became abusive, I could have chosen for that to be the end of the conversation. What I had been doing prior was sitting with her, putting the verbal abuse aside, and giving her space. That wasn't working. She may have calmed down but continued her pattern of lashing out when upset, even though she knew that lashing out was not who she wanted to be. What makes figuring out what is loving so confusing is often the most loving thing, provokes negative emotions. The client was not happy when I set that boundary; she didn't want to feel abandoned or rejected and acted out. But by allowing the client to abuse me, verbally was more hurtful to both of us in the long run. By setting the boundary, what was coming up was the client's fears, and that is the real work.

Chapter Three

Past Programming

Why do we struggle and suffer in the first place? How come some people seem to get all the worst luck while others have it easy? To answer these questions, let's start with birth. From in the womb to about seven or eight years old, you are most often in what is called *theta brain wave*. There is *beta* that is awake and interacting with the world around you. Then there is *alpha*, which is light meditation, and *theta*, which is deep meditation. You go into theta at least twice a day, every day. We hit theta just before falling asleep and just as we wake up. Theta has been referred to as *awake dreaming* and is when you can have vivid visualizations but are still fully awake. In studies on theta brain wave, it has been shown we are like sponges and learn much more quickly.

This is why children have such vivid imaginations and are like little sponges absorbing everything around them. After theta is *delta*, delta is sleep. There are also *gamma waves*, and studies have shown this is what people are in when they get spiritual or psychedelic like experiences when meditating. Monks are very good at getting into gamma. For now, we are going to discuss theta.

As you are likely aware, your brain was not fully developed when you were born. It doesn't get fully develop until about 25 years of age. Your frontal lobes are still developing as a child, and when you were under the age of eight, you didn't possess critical thinking ability. You were like a little sponge in constant hypnosis, absorbing everything around you. All of the information you were acquiring was creating the foundation for your subconscious, including all the beliefs about yourself and the world. It is not what happened to you that is the problem; it's how you perceived what happened to you, and children are quite egotistical. For children, the world is very *me*-centered. If one of your parents was having a bad day and lost their temper yelling at you for a mess you made, chances are good you took that to mean something was wrong with you. As a child, you were not able to understand or rationalize that your mother was possibly having a rough day and needing some time to relax. Instead, you most likely took it to mean that you were not loved when you made a mess or when you live up to what others wanted. This is a straightforward example and, when occurring once, is generally not a big deal; but happening again and again, and it becomes a different story. Now imagine you lost a parent in some way, whether it be through divorce or death or you were bullied at school or had a parent who physically abused you, or you had a sibling with issues that took up most of your parents' time and attention. The possibilities can go on and on and can cause a child to build a great deal of limiting and unloving beliefs about oneself and the world. Around the ages of seven or eight, you started to develop your critical mind, which means not everything went into your subconscious without thinking more critically about it. This does not mean that you could not still become traumatized; you just weren't a sponge absorbing it all without critical thinking. The critical mind is also why we can struggle at times to change our belief system. It tends just to throw out anything that isn't already in alignment with one's subconscious beliefs. Frustrating right? Don't worry; keep reading. There are ways around this.

So why does this matter, and what does it mean? It means that how you perceive and experience the world today is directly connected to the belief system you created as a child. We all have a degree of post-traumatic stress disorder. Maybe not to the level that is disrupting your life, but enough that you feel stuck in creating the change you want in life. Have you ever had an experience when you had an emotional reaction that seemed much stronger than called for by the situation? Or, have you ever been around someone who was responding to something with intense emotion, more than was necessary for the incident? You most likely even thought, *Boy, this person is acting like a child.* This is because our brain has stored all our memories, and its main job is to keep us alive. At the base level, the brain understands the present based on the past. When something upsetting happens to you, the mind is triggered to recall a disturbing past event. Remember when I said it's not what happened to us that is the problem, but how we perceive what happens to us? Research shows that up to 50% of what we remember might be incorrect. It gets distorted, generalized, and deleted based on how you perceive what is happening. You don't have to be conscious of this at all. Our subconscious is controlling about 95% of our functioning. When you walk, you aren't thinking *consciously* about the actual steps and strides you are taking; you just walk. You don't have to think about your heart beating; it just beats. That's your subconscious. It also is in control of most of your choices. Our conscious selves only get about five percent of our cognitive activity. Have you ever tried to break a habit and struggled to do so? Did you find yourself self-sabotaging over and over? This is because the subconscious is in control, and if you believe that the change you want will cause pain or suffering, your subconscious will stop it from happening, no matter how bad you want it. This is why willpower isn't enough. An example you may consider is when, as a child, you gave a presentation in front of your classmates and made a hugely embarrassing mistake. The entire class laughed at you, and you felt mortified. Today every time you attempt to give a presentation at work, you freeze up. This behavior holds you back from moving forward in your career. No matter how bad you want to move forward, you continue to find yourself frozen in fear when attempting to give a presentation in front of others. What is needed here is to shift the subconscious belief that presenting in front of others is dangerous. This book will help you understand how to shift your thoughts by changing past programming.

Your brain has not evolved to push you towards achieving goals and putting yourself in unknown situations. Even though we have the compacity to do that, your brain will encourage you to stay safe. Your brain is wired to keep you alive. It does this by encouraging you to stick with what is familiar and expend as little energy as possible. Think about that for a moment. When you do something new and unknown, your mind can not predict what might happen. That is not conducive to staying alive. Your mind sends you signals to stop what you are doing and go back to the familiar. Anxiety is a common emotion that is telling you you are afraid of the future. Depression, on the other hand, tends to be connected to regrets of the past, which is your mind attempting to find ways to avoid pain and stay alive. The problem many of us are often falling into is that we believe our thoughts. If it pops into our head, it must be true. Most people are not taught how to pause and question their thoughts. Many people spend most of their time in beta brain waves. We are focused outside of ourselves, looking to the world to make ourselves feel better. When things change, we will be happy. There are plenty of stories from people who got what they wanted and were still unhappy. The external is not the problem when it comes to happiness or unhappiness. As I mentioned earlier, it is not what happened *to you,* which is the problem; it is how you perceived it. Think of a computer. You could put stickers on your computer, change the case the computer came in, but you are not going to have a computer that operates differently until you change its programming.

Knowing this can help you be more empathetic with yourself. You are not broken. You may have had some horrific things happen in your life, and you might have taken those things to mean you are less than others, worthless, or unlovable, but that is unhelpful programming. The good news is you don't have to change the world to feel better. All you have to do is change yourself. It comes down to a simple choice; it is a choice that you will make repeatedly, but this choice is the key to experiencing a completely different life than you are now. This choice is the key to peace, happiness, joy, and ease. Are you ready to choose to love and accept all parts of yourself? Remember, just because you choose to accept all parts of yourself doesn't mean you are suddenly good at it. Kind of like if you decide to learn a new language. When you choose to learn that language, do you suddenly know the language? Of course not. What you are doing is setting your intention announcing to yourself: *This is what I am going to focus on, and I'm going to focus on it until I master it.* I will give you tools that can transform your life, but the tools are only useful when choosing to use them.

Chapter Four

The Observer

Let's talk more about the mind. Remember, when I said many people fall into the trap of believing their thoughts? Well, that includes you. I haven't met a single person who isn't guilty of doing this at least a thousand times a day. Our brain is pumping out about 60,000 thoughts in a day. How often are you stopping to question each thought? Our ego loves storytelling and drama. What is the ego? That is the part of your brain that identifies you as a personality. I am outgoing, shy, love animals, and so on. To start simple, let's split the brain up into two parts. You have more than that, but I don't want to overwhelm you. You have the ego, the part that identifies yourself as an *I*. The ego sees yourself as having different traits. These traits often come from our upbringing. We were not born with many of them. Let's say you struggled with making friends in school, and this struggle caused you to withdraw from others. Based on this behavior, you received feedback from adults that you were shy. You were likely told this often enough that it became a part of your identity. As you grew up, you saw yourself as shy. That would be the *ego* part of yourself. You don't have to be shy. You can be just about anything you want. Sure, there are some limitations, but there is way more possibility than constraints. Focusing on the limits only holds you back. It keeps you stuck. If the ego is one part of two, what is the other part? As you have probably guessed, it's the *observer.* Some people would call this part their higher self or soul self. However, I will keep it to the observer as that is what this part tends to do, observe. This is the part that can hear you reading these words right now. Our observer self is separate from our personality. This is the part that holds potential.

The best analogy I can offer is watching a movie. Think about when you were last in the movie theater watching a fantastic film. It was so good, and you forgot you were in a theater. Now consider the movie is your ego, and you in the theater are the observer. The movie isn't you, but you were able to forget about yourself and get absorbed into the film. I'll go a little deeper as I want you to really understand this. Now imagine we had the technology that you could choose to experience a character in the movie. Let's say it is an action movie, and you select the main character who has fighting skills. With our latest technology, you can put on goggles that put you into the mind of the character. You get to play the movie out through the character's eyes and traits. It is so real it's like you have the fighting skills. You can feel the adrenaline and excitement! You would forget you had the goggles on, wouldn't you? It would be like becoming another person. That is until the movie ended, and you took the goggles off. The observer is the part of you that is watching this experience of life.

Why is this important? The ego loves drama and is limited. The ego creates a story and lives within that story, similar to believing *I am shy; I have anxiety, I'm not good enough*. Some of the things the ego believes are useful and helpful, and you don't want to lose them. Some helpful beliefs include ones like *I like helping others* or *I am disciplined.* Other things are holding you back and are worth letting go of, such as *I'm not smart enough, I don't deserve good things*. As you learn the tools to start to change the relationship with yourself, you will find it works best when you can see that the story you are telling yourself is just a story. Being aware that you are the observer allows you to begin to question and challenge the beliefs that hold you back. When you become aware that you are the observer, not the ego, you get into a state of curiosity. You cannot be traumatized and curious simultaneously, and this is very important to note. It is the same as not being anxious and relaxed at the same time. When something is happening to you, and you define it as bad, you will experience it as bad. When you are in a state of curiosity, you have not labeled the event yet, leaving possibilities open. I think one of my favorite memes implies that when something goes wrong in your life, yell *plot twist* and move on. You don't know if something will be good or bad as you don't get to see the future. Being an observer and leaving the door open to possibilities allows those possibilities to enter into your life. Once you choose something, you have narrowed your focus and what we focus on we experience. Take a moment, stop reading, and for one minute, look around the room you are in and notice whatever is orange. Go ahead, take a minute, memorize everything orange, and come back to the book. Good. Now, tell me, what was blue? Wait. What?! You weren't focused on blue, were you? You were focused on orange, so you overlooked the blue items. Tony Robbins often remarks that where focus goes, energy flows. The more you practice the concept of seeing your life and actions as if in a movie theater watching a movie, the easier it is to let go of that which is not serving you.

This being a big topic, allow me to answer some questions that may have popped up for you. You may be asking if I am not my personality, then who am I? A book could be written on this question alone, and many already have. To keep it simple: you are limitless. You are potential. You are everything and nothing at the same time. You are in the theater and have access to experience any movie you want. As you start to understand this, you will discover that you have preferences. You may not be your ego or personality, but you did choose to step into this theater and experience the movie, and you will enjoy certain movies over others. The exciting news is you can create your movie. With the power of imagination, and the ability to step back and observe, you are not limited to your original programming. Let me share a story of a man who demonstrates this point.

Today, a man who is a successful magazine entrepreneur was not successful back in high school and was, in fact, failing. A single mom was raising him, and because of his family situation, he figured he wasn't smart enough to go anywhere in life and decided there was no point in trying. His mother wanted him to take the SATs and get into college, and so he took them. When he received his scores, they were in the 1400s, an extremely good score. He was shocked, and so was his mother. She wanted to know if he had cheated. He told her no, he hadn't. This young man was in his last year of high school, and after obtaining his scores, he started to think that maybe he was smart after all, and decided to start attending classes and focus on his studies. His teachers, who assumed he wasn't intelligent, felt guilt over how they had misjudged this young man. They began to make an extra effort to help him. When it came time to graduate, he was not in a position to get into an Ivey-league college because throughout his earlier years in high school, he hadn't applied himself, and that was reflected in his final grades. Instead, he decided to attend a community college.

From there, with time and effort put in, he was able to go on to an Ivey-league college, graduate, and eventually became an extremely successful magazine entrepreneur. You may say this all worked out because this man was intelligent. Well, here's the plot twist. About 12 years later, he got a letter from the SAT college board after a random audit on SAT scores. He opened the letter and came to discover that all those years ago, he had received someone else's score. His real score was in the 700s. This now very successful business entrepreneur didn't become successful because he was more intelligent than most; he was successful because he behaved like he was. This demonstrates the power of one's story and focus.

Another great question you may be asking is how to know if you are in ego versus observer role. Simply put, the ego believes the observer is curious about the thoughts of the individual. The observer is in a state of awareness. The ego is run by the programming of the brain and operates on autopilot. Your mind is like a Ferrari with a GPS (autopilot) and a driver (the observer). You can live your life on autopilot, but you never really get to see what your Ferrari (mind) can do. Once you realize you can take this beautiful piece of machinery off autopilot, do you think you will be an expert driver? Of course not! It will take practice. Would practicing be worth it? How curious can you be about what this beauty can do? Science used to think we were subjected to our genes. Then epigenetics was discovered, and now we understand that our environment is what turns our genes on and off. You have control here. There is a choice. Just because there is genetics in your family for Alzheimer's, does not mean you are doomed to this disease. The environment is not just what you eat, and where you live, it is also what you think and how you feel. The relationship with yourself is more important than you may have ever imagined.

There are hurt and pain in this world and horrible things happen. We cannot change that of which we are not aware. What is helpful is when you become aware of how you have defined yourself and your life before an effective and sustainable change can happen. Yes, there are horrors in this world, but there is also wonder, beauty, and awe, and they can all exist simultaneously. You have more choices than you may have thought initially. Of course, there are some limits in this world, but there is so much more potential than there are limits. To focus on your limits (the *ego-self*) only keeps you stuck there. To discover who you are is to open up to possibilities. I cannot tell you who you are. You already have that answer within you, and with some help, you can start to uncover it.

Chapter Five

Resistance

Let's talk about what resistance is, as it is essential in understanding to have this work go smoothly. I do not think resistance is actually resistance. Recall earlier when I mentioned we have more than two parts to ourselves, other than ego and observer self. With that in mind, we can better understand what resistance is. A psychological theory called the Internal Family Systems Model (IFS) was created by Richard Schwartz. This theory's concept is that we have parts much like multiple personalities, and each part has a job. Each part's role is an attempt to keep the system from exposing or feeling emotional pain. These parts are often protecting a wounded inner child. This idea is similar to shamanism and soul retrieval; the belief that parts of our soul are fragmented when something traumatic happens to us. Trauma is anything that feels emotionally painful.

The brain tends to be very dramatic and turns most incidents into life and death. What is essential to understand here is as a baby, most things are life and death. If someone did not take care of you as a baby, you would have died. That includes feeling loved. As you grew up, you learned to feed yourself but still depended much on your caregivers for survival. Now, as an adult, your brain is still stuck in this life or death way of thinking. Your brain is wired for survival; it wants to move toward what feels right and away from what feels wrong. Let's say there is a woman who's mother, as she was growing up, was verbally abusive. The mother constantly put the child down, criticizing her and rarely giving her praise. The child's father showed her love but never stood up for her against the mother. He would just step aside or ignore when the child's mother was berating the child. As you can imagine, this would feel very emotionally painful to a child, and she would come to believe she was not good enough or lovable. Her father may have shown her love, but he never stopped his wife from harming her, so the child took that to mean she deserved it. Fragmentation of a wounded child starving for love and acceptance, but fearful of rejection began to occur.

As you can imagine, there is going to be a split starting here. A part of the little girl is going to be desiring and seeking love and approval. Another part will believe she is unlovable, taking on the voice of her mother. Later in adulthood, and we have a woman who is looking for love and acceptance and most likely will appear needy, as she wants love but does not know how to give it to herself and doesn't believe she deserves it. She would not be drawn to a partner that showed her love and acceptance because that is not what she is familiar with, because she has a part in her that continues telling her she is unlovable. What she is drawn to is a partner who is similar to her mother, abusive, or similar to her father, dismissive. If this woman attempted to tell herself she deserved more, there would be that part of her telling herself she didn't. If she found a partner that showed her genuine love, this love would feel uncomfortable; she would reject the partner. We only allow in as much love as we are willing to give ourselves. Externally this would be seen as resistance to finding a more loving relationship. The woman would continue seeking love and approval from someone who is not providing it. The fear of rejection for this woman is going to trigger the life or death belief because, as a child, if she had been thoroughly rejected, she would have been unable to support herself. Love is a basic survival need. As an adult, this would cause her to cling tighter to her partner in fear, which in turn would most likely cause them to push her away, increasing her fear.

Through our different experiences in life, we have created parts within ourselves that are managing the system within the mind that ultimately desire to experience happiness but will settle with staying alive. Some of our parts are helpful and get things done for us. Other parts not so much, as their jobs are to immediately rescue us from pain. You could have a part that drinks alcohol or eats food when you are stressed. The reason this is important to understand is all the parts have your best interest in mind. They all want to feel good or at least not be in unbearable pain. They are all attempting to keep some homeostasis. It may seem like they are trying to sabotage you, but if you spend a little time understanding and listening to them, you will discover they believe what they are doing is helping. The observer is not a part. The parts are within the ego. The observer is the authentic you, which is the *you* connected to your spiritual self. This may seem complicated to understand at first, but what it ultimately comes down to is the relationship with yourself. It is choosing to love and accept all parts of yourself, the ones you like and those you think you don't like. The observer is worthwhile understanding as our parts are limited in their capability to access all possibilities. Think of the observer as the CEO of the Internal Family System, the one who has the most knowledge, wisdom, and leadership skills. The observer is the one who can look at a situation with compassion and curiosity. The parts tend to get stuck in their limiting beliefs and, therefore, their roles. Together they make up the ego, and the ego is about habits and limiting beliefs. Don't worry. The ego can be changed.

What does this have to do with resistance? When you have a goal and find yourself struggling to achieve the goal, sabotaging yourself, that is an actively involved part. You have a part that is saying, *If you achieve this goal, something painful will happen, so I'm not going to let you do it.* What do you think that might look like internally? War, right? You may find yourself angry with yourself and begin arguing with yourself, attempting to use will power. But all that fails, which leads to feeling frustrated and hopeless. I am willing to bet you have had this kind of experience more than once. This is why the observer is important. When one part fights another part, you don't get anywhere. When the observer comes in and is curious about what is going on, you can get some answers. A question about how you are benefiting from staying where you are may conjure up an initial reaction that there is no benefit; that would be a part. The observer would be curious and sit with that question. Changing the relationship with yourself is deciding to get on your team. Chances are, you have been fighting and putting yourself down for years now. I have not said this yet, but it is very important to understand: *acceptance does not mean you have to like it.* You can absolutely feel frustrated with where you are in life. This is not about ignoring your emotions or pretending to feel something you don't. This is about opening up to the possibility that there is a solution here you just haven't yet found. You have a choice of how you would like to handle whatever problem is at hand. You can put yourself down and fight with yourself over it. Or you can choose to become curious about yourself and your fears, opening up to the possibility that they are valid. As with the woman in the example, her fear of rejection is incredibly valid, given her childhood experience. Getting annoyed with her for sticking with an abusive partner isn't going to change anything. What needs to change is the belief that she is not enough and unlovable. What I am getting at is you can throw logic at resistance all you want, but it's not going to change it. It is like trying to throw a bouncy ball through the wall, just going to bounce right back to you. You need to understand that your resistance has valid points, even if you don't know right now from where they came.

How do I know if a certain *part* is expressing itself? If you have an emotion that is anything other than compassion or curiosity, a part is conveying itself. The observer is not a part. As Internal Family Systems view it, it's your Self with a capital *S*. Many theories have viewed it as the higher self, the soul self, even the I AM. I bet you're saying, *Holy crap! I'm in a part all the time*! Yep. Stepping into the observer takes practice. But first comes awareness and knowledge, which is what we are focused on right now. The principal first important and never-ending step is to become aware – to notice you are in a part. Start slow. All you have to do is acknowledge you are in a part. Begin to observe it. A great question to ask yourself is, *What do I have to believe about myself and the situation to feel this way*? This is a journey of discovering who you currently are in order to become who you truly are. Once you start noticing and asking yourself questions to understand yourself better, you have become the observer. Congratulations!

I will give you another useful tool to see if you are in a resistant part versus observing and accepting. When you are in resistance, your body will feel tight and heavy. It is like you are uncomfortably being squeezed, and the impulse will be to get out of the discomfort. When you start to observe, natural acceptance of the moment will come with this, and your body will begin feeling lighter and more expansive. You have just switched yourself from lower negative emotions such as anger, sadness, or frustration to a higher, lighter state. I like to ask myself, borrowed from Hale Dwoskin's book *The Sedona Method*, when I am in negative emotion, to consider, *Would I rather be in this emotion, or would I rather be free*? It is a simple question in helping you switch from autopilot to observing. Often when I ask myself that question, I feel my body tense and hold tighter to the emotion. This isn't a bad thing. It just means there is something here I can learn. Emotions are just messengers. You deserve to take the time to listen to yourself. This is where inner child work will come more into play. I will show you how to listen to yourself to create change in the next chapter.

Chapter Six

Rescue Yourself

In this chapter, I will teach you about inner child work, how to do it, and why it works. There are many tools available to help you release emotional pain, change your perspective, and experience healing. Inner child work is, by far, my favorite type of healing work. Do you remember when I mentioned before that we all have a form of post-traumatic stress disorder? Things happened to us as children that were emotionally painful. The brain took a snapshot of each painful moment and created a bit of a trauma loop in an attempt to avoid experiencing that pain again. Your brain perceives the current moment based on the understanding of the past. Studies even show that your state of being affects what information you take it. What this means is if a bunch of pictures is rapidly shown to a group of people, those who are depressed will notice and remember the sad pictures versus those who are not depressed. You perceive the world through a filter that has been created from your past experiences and current thoughts. Inner child work is a way to change your perception of what happened and change your relationship with yourself.

Let's just get straight to it, and I will explain its benefits as we go. Consider, hypothetically, or in reality, having a fight with your partner and feeling angry and hurt. Here is how you do inner child work. I want you to sit in those feelings of hurt and anger and just notice them. Where do you feel them in your body? Or maybe they are outside your body? If it had a shape and color, how would that feeling look? What I want you to do here is to become very familiar with the emotion. I don't want you to feed it by focusing on what happened or justify why you should be feeling this way. If those thoughts come up, you can notice them and let them pass. I want your focus on just noticing and becoming familiar with the emotion. After a couple of minutes of this, ask yourself, *When is the first time I can remember feeling this way*? Many people want to think hard here. No hard thinking is required. Just put the thought out there and let your subconscious do the work. A memory will come up. This aspect of the exercise does require patience; if you find yourself pushing to find the memory, you will notice it is harder to find a memory. If you let go and just accept that a memory will come when it comes, that memory will appear much faster. Once a memory comes to mind, you can ask yourself, *Is this the first time I felt this feeling*? The answer may come in a direct yes or no thought, or it may come in as a sense of yes or no. If you get no, you can let go of that memory and go back to when it was the first time you felt this way. This can be fun, at least I think so as I find it amazing that when I talk to my subconscious, it talks back to me. Frequently people will get a memory as a teen or even a young adult. You can use inner child work with yourself at any age, but I encourage you to start with finding a memory of a younger age. My reason behind this is we are often much more compassionate with our child self than our adult selves. Once you do this technique repeatedly, you will build that compassionate relationship with yourself, and you will find that you can be compassionate with yourself at any age.

Now that you have found the memory, as you look at the memory, I want you first to notice how you feel looking at your younger self. It is important here that you have empathy and compassion when you look at yourself. If you have some other emotion, ask that emotion just to take a step back until you feel more gentle feelings toward yourself. I want you to look at the memory and notice similar feelings your younger self is having from any current event that just happened. Remember, our mind only remembers only about 50% of what happened. The rest of the mind improvises, often based on how you perceive the situation, so don't worry about how accurate this memory is. It doesn't matter. It is more important we work with how the mind interpreted it than actual facts. I tell you this because you might come up with a memory of being physically hurt by another and think it's true. Perhaps a memory of one of your parents hitting you pops up, but you have never remembered this before. It does not mean your parent did hit you, but as a child, it may have felt so emotionally, and your brain is now expressing this symbolically to you. Our subconscious speaks in symbolism. Dreams are a great example of this.

The next step is to ask your younger self to share with you whatever he or she wants. Here we are just allowing the child to unburden themselves. Let them express to you what they were thinking and feeling from this event. Just nod and let them know you are listening and hearing them. See what they learned about themselves and the world from this event. Other memories may pop up. Just notice them and let the memory pass; we want to work entirely with the first memory before moving onto a second. After your younger self has expressed all they need, the next step is to validate them. This is a *very* important step. The most common impulse is to want to jump in with logic and tell the child, *You'll be ok, your parent doesn't hate you*, or so on. Try it, and you'll find success, I am certain. After you attempt to change your younger self's feelings with logic, check in, and see how they respond. I can guarantee you that they will still feel bad, maybe even worse. That's because when you jump in with logic, as accurate as it may be, it is invalidating the child's emotions, and no one likes ing told what they are feeling is wrong.

Validation is one of the most important steps, and I'm going to spend some time explaining it. Validating feelings does not mean you confirm the child's beliefs, such as you are right that your dad hated you. You are just accepting and confirming their emotions. Of course, if this happened to you, it may have felt like your parent hated you because screaming and yelling does not feel loving. Perhaps you were sent to your room, resulting in feeling hurtful and rejecting. I can understand why you would have been confused and angry; your parent didn't take the time to teach you about your behavior, seeming just to expect you to know. And, if this happened to you in reality, I am so sorry you experienced it, and you felt this way. The more time you take here, validating your younger self, the more powerful it can be. As you validate, check in with your younger self. He or she will start to feel lighter and better. That means you are doing a good job. What you are doing here is releasing the trapped emotional energy. When something hurtful happens, and we aren't able to process it, it gets stuck. Letting your younger self unburden and then you as an adult validates the emotions is a huge step in letting go. I tell my clients this process is like going back in time and rescuing themself. You know that you are just using imagination, but science shows your brain does not know the difference between real or imaginary. Want proof? Have you ever felt anxious about something that had not happened? Just the thought of it happening created anxiety.

Once you have validated your younger self and he or she is feeling lighter and better, now it's time to keep building a trusting relationship. If there was another person in the memory that harmed you in some way, I want you to tell that person off. Think of it this way, go back in time and stand up for this child that had no one to stand up for them before. Here it is okay to be angry. Express yourself, let it out. Here you are unburdening. What you are also doing is building trust with yourself as you are standing up for yourself. You are showing yourself that you have your back, your feelings matter and that you are worthy and deserving. When you start doing inner child work, you may find that your younger self does not trust you. This is normal because, let's be honest, in the past, you haven't been very nice to yourself as you could have been. You are going to have to prove to yourself, just like you would have to prove to anyone else, that you do care about yourself. If you are still struggling with feeling care for yourself, it is back to that original choice that you will make over and over. You can tell yourself *I choose to love and accept all parts of myself, light and dark*. Remember, it is like choosing to learn a new language. Just because you choose it doesn't mean you now know the new language. Your choices set your intention and keep it there. You learn as you practice.

Once you have, in the memory, expressed your emotion and told off the person that hurt you, I want you to ask your younger self what else he or she needs from you at this moment. If the answer is yes, provide it. It might be to hold that child, to listen some more; it might just be your child self asking questions. Be there for your child self. Once that is complete, or your younger self says there isn't anything else needed, I want you to ask if they are ready to leave this memory. If you get a no, explore what else needs to be finished in this memory. It is done and over, and your child self does not need to stay there anymore. When your child self answers, they are ready to leave this memory, I want you to bring your child self to the present and show him or her everything you have in your life that you love. It doesn't matter how small it is or may appear. What we are doing here is syncing up the brain; the part that holds the memories does not understand linear time and can get stuck in time loops. Believe it or not, there is a part of you that still thinks you are a child and stuck with child options. By bringing your younger self to the present, you link the past to the present and let your brain know you are not a child.

Once you have done this, check in with your younger self again. If you haven't noticed yet, checking in with your younger self is valuable, and there is benefit from being done often. You are looking to see how your subconscious feels and what shifts may need to be made. If your younger self is still doing good, you can ask him or her if they are ready to let go of the past. Are they prepared to let go of the hurt and pain? If they say no, explore why. What bad might happen if they let go? There might still be some validation and acceptance that needs to be done here. If your child self still does not want to let go, that is okay. You will be checking in with them later, and when he or she is ready, they will let go. If you get an indication that your child self is willing to let go, ask them how they would like to release their hurt or pain. It will often be related to one of the four elements – earth, water, air, or fire. They might bury it, let waves carry it away, release it in a balloon or want to burn it. The possibilities of how this may be experienced are endless. Allow your child self to decide. Once this is done, ask them where they would like to stay, anywhere of their choosing that is safe, real, or imaginary. Once they decide, imagine them there with whatever else they may want, including friends, toys, or animals. Then place that special place in your heart, acknowledging that your child self knows they are with you always, and you are taking care of them.

After you have done this entire process, it is important to check in with your child self every day for the next week. The reason behind this is that you are building new synaptic connections. By checking in with your child self, you make the connections you have already built stronger and more solid. If you don't do this step, your brain can return to its old connections, and you'll find your younger self back in the memory repeating the trauma loop. When you check in with your child self, you are seeing if there is anything they need from you. If they weren't ready to let go of the hurt, you could ask them if they are ready now. Often our child selves just want to know that we have not forgotten them. They simply want to know that we love and accept them. Even as adults, we never get tired of hearing that we are loved and accepted just as we are. And if no one has ever expressed love and acceptance to you just as you are, the best place to start is with yourself!

To summarize the steps, you first want to get a feel for the emotional reaction, then ask yourself when the first time was that you felt this way. When a memory comes up, listen to your younger self until they have nothing more to share, and then validate all their emotions. And remember that the next step is an important one: you want to validate the emotions because if you don't validate them and just try to explain why they should feel differently, it will feel like you are trying to throw a rubber ball through a wall. It is just going to bounce back. Once you have fully validated your child self, you stand up for yourself. This is building a trusting relationship with yourself. I tell people they may think they don't want something bad to happen outside of themselves, but that isn't the real issue. The real issue is how you treat yourself when something bad happens. That is what you are trying to avoid. That is what you want to change and have the power to change. After you stand up for yourself and check in again with your younger self, ask if they are ready to leave the memory. When they respond affirmatively, bring them to the present to sync up your brain. Our brain is like a computer program, and we want to keep the program updated. After showing your younger self all the things in life you love and are grateful for, ask your child self if they are ready to release the hurt and pain. Then allow them to release that hurt or pain through one of the four elements. From there, put them in a safe place of their choosing, set that safe place in your heart, and check in on them every day for the next week.

Chapter Seven

Integration

Knowledge is power, and understanding why you want to do this technique will help you follow through on it. The key to healing is integration. What is integration? In a nutshell, it is choosing to love and accept all parts of yourself, light and dark. As a kid, I was very sensitive to negative energy. I felt it around me often. It would wake me up at night, putting me in states of frozen fear. I used many techniques I had heard about to try to protect myself. I would squeeze my eyes shut and surround myself with white light, but nothing seemed to work. I was plagued with darkness. Then one day, through some spiritual readings and research, I came across the concept that everything is a reflection of oneself. I'll be honest, I am still coming to understand what that means, but once that concept was introduced into my reality and I started to play with what it could mean, I came to wonder if all the darkness I had experienced was a reflection of me as well. My initial reaction to this was a resounding no! Honestly, how many people are going to embrace that there may be darkness within them? How many would acknowledge that there may be war and violence within them? If you are anything like me, you want to believe and feel that you are good. You don't want war and violence! Here is the key: it is not about wanting it. I don't want it either. I also didn't want to experience the darkness, but maybe having the potential is different than wanting. After all, if someone were harming a person I loved and cared about, wouldn't my instinct be to protect them? Even to the point of maybe hurting that person. Here is where your brain may want to justify the behavior. Well, that is different. It's okay to defend. The person I am harming may not think it's okay. Marvel comics seem to do a great job of explaining this. Often the *bad guy* doesn't think they are the bad guy. But we define them like that because of what they are willing to do to achieve what they want. But then isn't the *good guy* doing the same thing? Aren't they both willing to hurt to achieve what they want?

Some of my favorite movies are the ones that explain the background of the bad guy. Take, for example, the film *Maleficent*[1] with actress Angelina Jolie. If you haven't seen it, it's a must to see, and I'll try not to ruin it completely, but here is your spoiler alert warning. It is about the evil witch in sleeping beauty. Angelina Jolie plays the witch, and the story explains how she becomes evil. Jolie's character starts as a kind and loving fairy who falls in love with a man, a poor man, who is also a kind person but desires to have riches and live in the kingdom and not a barn. His desire to feel better outweighs his love for the kind and loving fairy, and when he gets an opportunity to be the king's successor, he takes it. Only he cares for her, so instead, he doesn't quite do what the king demands but still very damaging to the kind and good fairy.

I think just about anyone would agree that the fairy is justified in her anger at what happens to her. And the once kind and loving fairy lets anger take her over. She feeds it every day, and it becomes a big part of her personality, turning her into an evil witch. This movie is an excellent example of what happens to us is not our fault, but how we respond is our responsibility. I'll get to that later because what I want to point out first is we all have the potential to allow negative emotions to take us over, becoming "evil," in a sense. It may not be what you prefer. Even though it's just fiction, I still think it is safe to say the fairy never preferred becoming an evil witch. The pain of betrayal was so great, and the subconscious used anger and revenge to wield its power.

So, what is integration? Integration is allowing the existence of your pain and hurt. When something emotionally painful happens to us, the brain's job is to protect us from that happening again. It takes a snapshot of the event and then keeps an eye out for anything that looks remotely similar. This is all done subconsciously. You don't even have to think about it. The problem is that it keeps you in survival mode: fight or flight. You continue to repeat the same patterns. When you continue to feel the same emotion over and over, such as Jolie, in her movie character's anger, we create more receptor sites on our cells for that emotion. Our bodies become used to the emotion, and when we are not feeling the emotion, our body will send signals back to the brain, telling it to create the emotion! Your body becomes the subconscious, wanting to stay in homeostasis. To change this, we first have to become aware of our patterns, our programming. By noticing our feelings and doing inner child work, we are improving our awareness. We are also starting to integrate, which means instead of running from the painful event because it hurt and at the time may have been difficult to explain. When we sit with our younger self and let them express what they could not at the time, we are allowing all to exist, no longer fighting it or resisting it. This is integration. This is choosing to love and accept all parts of ourselves, light and dark. This is acknowledging that all potential exists within. The goal is not to deny it or try to cut it off. That is impossible. It is to observe it as a valid option. Just because it is an option, does not mean it is you or that you have to choose it. When you resist something, you have your attention on it, and giving your attention to something gives it power.

Integration is the opposite of resistance. It is allowing everything to exist. Integration is not always easy as most of us spend our lives trying to avoid pain. Pain is real, and suffering is a choice. I will remind you that it is not what happens to us that is the problem but how we perceive what is happening to us. By sitting with your younger self, you allow that part of you to feel all the emotions that are already there without shame, guilt, or blame. It just is. Once the emotions are allowed and no longer denied, you will feel lighter, larger. Integration is expansion. Learning is expansion. Inner child work is learning more about yourself and who you prefer to be.

When you step back and see that all exists and you can choose what you prefer, that is freedom. Choosing to love and accept all parts of yourself, light and dark, is stating that you understand that you are potential. All options are valid. You are both light and dark. Both options are there. There will be times in your life that you choose the dark option. This is okay. Our choices are not a reflection of who we are; it is just a reflection of what we choose. Maleficent wasn't an evil witch. She was making choices that caused her to look that way, and it was a valid option that she explored, but it wasn't her. She was all options.

When we integrate, we give ourselves the option to change our programming. By allowing all experiences to exist, without judgment, we can see what we prefer. Once I learned that even this darkness, which I would experience often, was a reflection of potential in me, I chose love. I would state in my mind, *I understand that this is a reflection of something inside of me, and I choose to love and accept all parts of myself, light and dark*, and I would feel love toward wherever that part was. I didn't need to know where it was. Simply choosing love changed my experience. I allowed the darkness to exist. I didn't need to fight it, which freed up my energy to focus on my preference: love and acceptance.

Let's talk about the symptoms of not integrating. You may feel like you keep pulling the same kind of people into your life, ones that hurt you. You may feel like you are out of control of your emotions and choices. You set goals and sabotage yourself. You find yourself carrying out unhealthy behaviors to avoid feeling certain emotions or in an attempt to feel better. You may feel stuck or lost in life. The list goes on. When you don't integrate, one could say you are segregated. You have parts of yourself separated and locked up because it feels unsafe to feel them. When that part is opened up, you have an impulsive behavior to lock it back up, such as anger outbursts, drinking, eating, shopping, drug use, isolation, overworking; you most likely understand what I mean. It takes a lot of energy and effort to keep parts of ourselves separated and hidden.

You might be doing this because you fear deep down that it is all true, and maybe you are worthless. I am going to tell you a secret: your worth is inherent. You were born with it. You can know this by looking at a baby. A baby has worth and needs to do nothing to earn it and cannot lose it. The idea of worthlessness is just an idea or opinion, but not the truth. No one, not even you, can decide your worth. With the power of our minds, it sure can seem like ourselves or others get to determine our worth, but it is an illusion. Fear of being worthless is keeping yourself segregated. You weren't born with that fear. It came from somewhere. Maybe you were told it, maybe lots of little things happened to you that caused you to interpret it that way. Choosing to feel worthless is a valid option. As valid as choosing to feel worth. When you sit down and take the time to feel your feelings, observe and validate them, you are integrating. You are, in a way breaking down all the energy walls that are holding your potential at bay. It becomes one beautiful field of possibility. It feels like flow. Suddenly the options in your life become limitless. Or at least nearly limitless. Why focus on the limits when there is so much potential?

Chapter Eight

How to Let Go

Continuing with all possibilities existing within oneself, what you focus on is what you will experience. When we hold limiting beliefs and fears, that is where we are giving our energy. It is as if you are telling your brain, *Hey, look for these things.* The brain listens to what you tell it, and it will look for those fears and limiting beliefs. As humans, we tend to look for proof of what we believe. Even when those beliefs feel like crap, there is comfort in finding their existence. It feels dependable. You may feel awful, but at least you don't feel out of control. If you believe that you stink at a skill, whatever it may be, your brain focuses on that and finds the proof of it. It may be people telling you so, and it may be just yourself telling you.

Either way, you say to yourself, *See! I was right! Phew! The world is stable again.* When we are in a state of new or unfamiliar, our body becomes out of homeostasis and wants to revert to what is familiar. It will give this feedback to your brain, and thoughts will encourage you to hold on to your current beliefs. This is why it is so difficult for so many to change. We don't like sitting in discomfort. We project our fears into the unknown, and the body and brain scream to go back to the familiar, even if that is miserable. Your body and brain are not against you; they're just constructed for survival. Going into the unknown can be dangerous whether we're looking at prehistoric, early, or modern man. Today, an example would be walking down a dark alley that you have never walked down before. Your brain and body are going to tell you, *We have no blueprint for this! Turn back; this could be dangerous!* But when it comes to changing our limiting beliefs and facing our fears, our body and brain's desire for survival becomes more of a roadblock than help.

When I am surrendering to fear, I go straight to the worst-case scenario. People will ask me, isn't that focusing on what you don't want? Yes, but your unconscious has already gone there, so you might as well acknowledge it. Remember when I said awareness is the first, most important never-ending step? You can't change what you don't know. Go to the fear and acknowledge its existence. Acknowledge its possibility. This is the same as validating yourself. If you approach it by telling yourself why you shouldn't feel or think that way, the fear won't subside. Go ahead and seriously give it a try. It is important to observe that when you try to convince yourself that you don't have a fear, it doesn't work. It is like the analogy I used before of trying to throw a rubber ball through a wall. It merely bounces right back and tends to feel like it hits you smack dab in the middle of the forehead. It can also feel like a rift or separation within yourself because it is. You are invalidating a part of yourself. How do you feel toward a person who tells you what you feel and thinks it is wrong? Do you tend to feel closer to them, or do you tend to feel yourself pull away? Pull away, right? No one likes being told what is going on in their head is wrong. It creates self-doubt and even a little crazy-making. What I want you to do instead is acknowledge that your fear is *one* possibility.

When you listen to the part of yourself that is fearful, I want you to be in the observer role. If you get thoughts or reactions that want to argue with your fearful self, just ask those thoughts to take a step back. Imagine yourself being a mediator. You are in a room full of people that want to be heard. If you allow everyone to speak at the same time, it will be chaotic. Take control and listen to each part one at a time. If another part jumps in, ask it to wait its turn. When I say parts, I mean emotional reactions and thoughts that might come up as you listen to your fears. It is helpful to refer to them as parts so you can get into the observer role, rather than feeling lost in the emotions. When you listen to your fears, if the thought pops in that this is stupid, you can acknowledge the thought and ask it to wait its turn. You have likely had the experience of feeling like you were arguing with yourself. This is what I mean by parts. We can have different desires at the same time. This is why getting into the practice of being the observer is so important. When you get highly emotional, you are not working from your frontal lobe, which is logic, reason, and will power; you work from the older parts of your brain, which focus on survival and fight, fight, freeze. Getting into the observer, that state of curiosity and compassion, keeps your frontal lobe processing.

Have you ever gotten upset and said or did something you later regretted? That is what I'm talking about. When you let the emotions take over, you are in old programming and patterns. You want to listen to the part of you that is fearful. That part deserves to be heard. Acknowledge that fear exists and validate the desire to stay still, to keep with the familiar. It is normal and makes sense. After you validate the part of you that is fearful, you will feel a slight energy shift. It feels good to be listened to, even if what you are saying might be irrational or extreme. It still feels good to be heard.

It is not so much what might happen to you that you fear, but how you will treat yourself if that incident happens. Your brain might tell you that you fear the event, but that is only because it sees that event as the trigger of any internal pain that may come from it. After you sit and validate the part of you that is fearful, commit to forgiving, and supporting yourself if that event is ever to happen. Think about this: if there was a risk you wanted to take but were scared to, and someone told you that they had your back and that no matter what happened, they would be there for you, accepting you, loving you, and giving you the comfort needed, do you think it would be a little easier to take that risk? Of course, it would. What I am telling you is don't abandon yourself.

Acknowledge that you are choosing to take a risk and that the risk *could* blow up in your face because you cannot promise yourself it won't. I strongly encourage you to never lie to yourself because lying to yourself is not a foundation for a good relationship. Acknowledge that a worst-case scenario is one possibility, and for some reason, if it happens, you won't shame yourself or put yourself down; you will support yourself and recognize the courage it took to take that risk. Choose to accept and love yourself for your existence, not your output. Of course, you are hoping for certain life experiences, but those experiences have no connection to your worth. You are worthy just for your existence. It is inherent. It is a birthright for everything in existence. Babies are not worried about their worth. The belief that we can lose our worth is a societal creation and a false one at that. You are back to choosing to love and accept all parts of yourself, light and dark, including what you enjoy and what you don't enjoy. Most people don't enjoy failing; those who do fail know it is just an element of success, learn from it, and quickly move past it. It is okay to acknowledge you don't enjoy certain experiences, but you will not accept those experiences as reflections of your worth. You understand that you make mistakes. Everyone does; it is a part of the learning process. Sometimes you can make huge mistakes. Your actions are not a reflection of your worth. They are a reflection of possibilities. Sometimes we choose a possibility that is out of alignment with our inner being. That is why it feels intuitively wrong. Punishing yourself for it will not help you learn. It will only cause you to feel worse. It is putting your energy and focus on feeling bad. When you make the really big mistakes, you make amends if you can, and you acknowledge this is not who you are or want to be, and you can ask yourself, *So who do I want to be*? We are all victims of victims. It is pain in ourselves that causes you to hurt another, be it emotionally or physically, so if you desire to help yourself and others, that means you need to let go of that hurt. Self-punishment does not bring you there. Choosing to love and accept all parts of yourself will.

Once you have committed yourself to love and accept yourself no matter what happens, now you can bring in logic. When part of your energy is tied up on focusing on what you don't want, you cannot fully use your power of focus to do what you want. By validating yourself and promising to support yourself, you free some of your negative energy, if not all of it, by letting go of resistance. That will allow you to take that extra energy and look at what you do want. Frequently this will be focusing on why you want to take a risk. It may be focusing on all the positives that could come from this risk, and most likely, it will be both.

I will use myself as an example in helping you understand this at a deeper level. When I decided to switch my business model, I had a fear of failure. I had been working for other partnerships and had a dependable and regular paycheck. In changing my business model by going out on my own into private practice, I lost that guaranteed income. I had no assurance that I would have enough clients to pay the bills. I had no idea if I would be successful or not. I could have plowed through telling myself what others were telling me, *I can do it, I'm skilled, it's easy*. I would say those things to myself, and most of them did not resonate with me at all because I had a part of me that did not believe it. Instead of allowing an internal argument and war, I got into my observer self and listened to the fearful part, asking it, *What is the worst-case scenario*? As soon as I asked the question, I had the answer. I thought that perhaps I might bomb, I would somehow not live up to my expectations for supporting clients, embarrass my family, ruin everything, and be homeless. I let my fearful part express herself. I validated that without a doubt, that would be a horrible experience. No wonder she wants to keep me safe. And of course, I agree with her; I didn't want to experience that either! But, if it were to happen, I promised not to blame or shame. I know that mistakes are part of the learning process and can feel painful. I promise to lovingly sit with myself in that hurt. If I were to fail in my new business model, I vowed to use that opportunity to build my relationship with myself. And even if there were to become a struggle with supporting myself, I promised to forgive myself for that too. As I could feel the energy shift happening within me, I felt a bit lighter. I brought into focus the reasoning for wanting to take this business risk, recognizing that I didn't want to live with regret. As Jim Rohn put it, "We must all suffer from one of two pains: the pain of discipline or the pain of regret. The difference is discipline weighs ounces while regret weighs tons." I may not be the most skilled therapist out there, but I do have skills, and I will continue to build my skills. I determined that I would rather look back on my life when I am 80 years old and know that I gave it my best even if I flailed at points along the way. Even if, like a fish out of water, I will know that I at least I tried. I believe that courage paves the way for others. That courage, that risk is what excited me. All I had to do was to take action. And, because I did, I prevailed! Succeeding now has just become the icing on the cake.

Chapter Nine

Reparenting Yourself

You may be noticing a theme here with how to sit with the part of you that is hurting. I titled this book *You Are Your Soulmate* because I firmly believe we are our first and most important soulmate. The relationship you have with yourself is going to affect and reflect your relationships with everyone else. So what is a soulmate? I don't mean soulmate as in just a partner. I believe we have many soulmates in our lives who play the role of partners, friends, and family. A soulmate is someone who connects not just to your personality, but your inner being: s—someone who knows and sees all of you. A soulmate is someone who sees you, supports you, and uplifts you on this journey of life. It's worth repeating: you are your first and most important soulmate. If you didn't know this before, you know this now.

Part of being a soulmate is providing for yourself what you needed and did not get. People can often make the mistake that if they did not receive what they wanted in the past, then it's too late. In this manner of thinking, they are a person who is then lacking. Don't fall into this trap. Maybe you didn't have two parents, and possibly your parents were not loving. You cannot change that, but you absolutely can change your perception of the past and provide for yourself the belief system you wish you had. This starts with reparenting yourself. Reparenting provides *for yourself* the boundaries, love, acceptance, and guidance you wish you had received. Reparenting is not always easy. If your parents were not good parenting role models, you will have to learn what a good parent is. When you are in the observer role, the good news is it comes easily because we know deep within what we wanted and what is best for us.

In this chapter, I want to cover the main themes in parenting that you will find yourself repeatedly doing. To start with, there is *validation.* You may be thinking that we already discussed validation. And you would be correct, yet it is so important a concept that I will examine it again. Validation does not mean you confirm limiting hurtful beliefs. It means you confirm the emotions. The emotions are where it is all at. The emotions are our guidance system in our state of being. This is why conscious manifestation seems so complicated; people are often trying to create something from a state of being that does not match what they want. Albert Einstein is given credit for the quote, "We cannot solve our problems with the same thinking used to create them." While this book is not on how to manifest material items, it is on how to manifest love of yourself. You cannot find love and acceptance for yourself if you invalidate yourself. Part of all of our pain and suffering is due to self-abandonment.

Every time you feel bad and attempt to change your state of being, you are abandoning a part of yourself. You are essentially saying that this feeling is not accepted, go away. Now externalize that and imagine what it would be like if someone told you, "I don't like who you are, go away." Maybe that has happened to you. Felt horrible, didn't it? A part of you may have tried to villainize the other person, but another part felt utterly rejected and abandoned. You most likely do this to yourself regularly, perhaps even daily. Then you wonder why you feel down in life when you may have so much about which to be happy.

Validation is valuable as it is part of that integration about which I previously discussed. Acceptance does not mean you like it. It means it just is. The first step on the road to health and wellness is listening and acknowledging that you feel hurt and suffering. I don't care how irrational it may seem in the moment. Remember, the brain understands the present based on the past. Somewhere in the past, it was logical and rational. Think about a small child who was made fun of at school and came home saying they had no friends. A parent who comes in thinking they are helping by admonishing that the child does indeed have friends is only invalidating that child's current perspective on reality. That child would not have felt accepted as they are.

Before you can go where you want, you must first acknowledge where you are. Validation of the child is not agreeing with the child that they are right and have no friends. You want to focus on the child's feelings as in showing empathy by saying, "You must feel so alone." When you reparent, you are doing the same thing with yourself. At one point, I worked for a suicide and crisis hotline. People would call in with pills in their hands, ready to end it all. Their lives had valid reasons for suffering, and often, it was a long list of things not going well. On the other end of the phone, the only real power I had was to listen and reflect on their feelings. I couldn't fix their lives or change their past. All I could do was acknowledge that they were in an internal hell right now and wanted it all to stop. I was always amazed at how just this little act of listening and validation could give a person so much peace and a willingness to face another day. Never underestimate the power of validation.

When you validate yourself, you stop fighting your feelings. You will feel the shift physically. Your body will go from being tight and heavy to lighter and expansive. Getting what we want in life is all about focus. When you invalidate yourself, your focus and energy are tied up in a battle of feelings. Once you stop fighting and accept your current feelings, you have freed the energy to shift to what you want. Going back to the child who stated they had no friends, after giving them the time to integrate their sadness, allowing the child to feel accepted no matter how they felt, that child could open to changing their perspective. I have a secret for you: you don't want to feel bad. Shocker, right? Even though we can get addicted to feelings, our cells make more receptor sites for the emotions we keep pumping out, and our brain likes what is familiar; ultimately, our conscious selves and our mind want to feel good.

The next recurring theme in reparenting is *self-discipline*. Because we can get addicted to emotions, and it takes time to teach the body a new homeostasis. Because the brain likes to move to what feels positive and satisfying, instant gratification is a challenge many of us have in life. What do you think a child would be like if their parents gave them everything they wanted? Horrible, right? They would also become an individual who could not handle sitting in discomfort and would likely end up abandoning themselves over and over again, as this is what the parents did to them in giving in to their every desire. When a child is in discomfort, and the parent does whatever they can to change that, that action signifies that discomfort is wrong or bad and that they cannot be with their child when they feel that way. This is the challenging part of reparenting. Knowing where you are in your discomfort or comfort is a necessary step, and so is knowing where you want to go. And where we want to go is often new, which means feeling some level of discomfort. You validate yourself, then set a boundary. You will make mistakes, I promise. Whenever we are learning something new, we have the potential to fail. It is a step in the process. Consider a toddler learning to walk. Should a parent shame the toddler every time they fall? If it seems like I am insulting your intelligence, I am not. I want to demonstrate that every time you get angry with yourself for a mistake made, it is similar to a parent shaming a toddler every time they fall while learning to walk. A toddler only knows that it needs to put one leg in front of the other, and yet they keep falling. It is that simple. As adults, we complicate our experiences by adding a story that tells us how we think our learning *should* look. As a toddler is learning to walk, they build muscle, and the brain is no different. It takes time to teach ourselves something new.

Let's explore an example of addiction. In this example, I will use alcohol, and even if you do not struggle with alcohol specifically, just allow your mind to see how struggling with any behavior you may not want could unfold this way. Imagine you aren't a casual drinker, but a daily drinker, and it has been causing problems in your life. You know that stopping is what is best for you. You know it is best for you, so it should be easy to quit, right? It can be if you let it, or it can be one of the most challenging things you have ever attempted. First, alcohol and most addictions are never the root cause;

they are a symptom of something else. Alcohol is a great way to avoid oneself and one's discomfort. The first step is exploring the triggers. Often anxiety is a trigger, and alcohol is used to increase the feel-good chemicals and shut down the frontal lobe. Once one of the emotions that trigger the desire to drink is uncovered, you can do inner child work: sitting with the emotion, letting it get familiar, and with that, you are beginning to integrate, allowing yourself just to be as you are. You can then ask yourself the first time you remember feeling this way. As the memories come up, you can reparent yourself for each and every memory. You can become familiar with the hurt you felt in the past and provide for yourself that loving accepting adult you wished you had. Each time you do this, the relationship with yourself becomes stronger and deeper. You are rebuilding trust in yourself, taking actions to show yourself that you matter and are important. Now comes the self-discipline. Your body and brain are in a pattern of reaching for alcohol when it feels the trigger of stress. Here you validate, then self-discipline, perhaps saying to yourself, *I know you want to drink, but that will not bring what we deeply desire.* You provide yourself the love and support you want and need. In this example, you would build other tools to help find relaxation. You wouldn't have to sit in your discomfort permanently, just long enough to show yourself you are not abandoning yourself, and you deserve to feel better. Each time you choose the direction you desire, you build self-confidence. The momentum becomes more robust, and it becomes easier. If you fall off the wagon, you can get right back on. Beating yourself up only gives you more reasons to drink or utilize whatever unhealthy method of escape you are attempting to quit. Just like that toddler who falls, there is no shame, guilt, or punishment. You can get back up and try again. It is that simple: treating yourself like you would want your very best friend, ultimate partner, a soulmate to treat you. With total loving acceptance and then a push in the best direction for you, your soulmate will never shame you for how long it takes. They will say it is just going to take as long as it takes. That is a great way to see how one's emotions are the guidance system. Should you fall off the wagon, you can tell yourself, *It's taking too long to quit. How does that feel? Rejecting, alone, not good enough, a failure, just plain yuck*. Now you fall off the wagon, and you can choose to tell yourself, *It's just going to take as long as it takes. Sure, it'd be nice if it was faster, but it will happen.* And that would feel better. The first scenario feels like it sucks your energy away, and the desire to give up could increase. That would be because you are focused on a negative belief, and the natural reaction could be to get away from the pain. In the second scenario, you don't deny your frustration, but you also aren't focused on limitations. It is a gentle shift of focus to what you really want, and that will feel better, pulling your brain in that direction. Remember, when I said in the beginning, these are just tools that will help get the brain to work for you? Tuning into one's emotions and listening to them can guide you to where you want to be.

Chapter Ten

Repetition Repetition Repetition

This chapter, the shortest in the book, is one of the most important. We learn by practice. That's it—chapter complete. I am being humorous, yet at the same time, it is that simple. This simple fact is also one of the biggest challenges. Since you don't get to see the fruits of your labor right away, giving up becomes a temptation. Being very clear on why you are doing this and mastering the skill of self-discipline becomes very important, so I will cover both in more depth.

Friedrich Nietzsche said, "He who has a why to live for can bear almost any how."[2] Since we become accustomed to feeling the same feelings and having the same beliefs, it becomes very uncomfortable when we try to change. Your body will desire to go back to its familiar even if the familiar is miserable, and your mind will give you thoughts pushing you to fall back into your old patterns. Knowing why you want to change is immensely important, especially to one's success. Let's use getting in shape as an example. You have decided that you want to lose some fat and put on muscle. Let's start with why you might desire that. Maybe you have been having aches and pains from sitting around and not getting much exercise. Perhaps you read how detrimental a sedentary lifestyle is to a person, and you need to take care of yourself. Maybe your clothes fit tight. Maybe you have been overall just not feeling your best, and you want to feel better. Take time to thoroughly understand the reason behind your desire and what feeling better could look like and feel. Then consider what it is going to take to get to where you want to be. Maybe you will sign up for a gym membership and get a trainer who gives you nutritional information and a personalized workout. You start out feeling excited about becoming the new you! You can see it in your mind, and you cannot wait to experience it. You faithfully go to the gym for the first week and throw out all the junk food in your house. Shortly after this, the discomfort starts to set in.

Lifting weights is challenging, and your body aches afterward. You have been lifting for a week, and you look the same in the mirror. You hurt, you're hungry, and so far, it seems like you feel worse than you did before. You begin wondering when the good feelings will appear? Lifting weights is a good analogy as most people understand that seeing muscle growth with the naked eye doesn't happen overnight; it takes a lot of repetition. Change and growth are happening on day one; that's why you're sore after the first day of lifting. Your muscles are torn down, and they rebuild themselves a little bit bigger and stronger, just not to the level that you can see with the naked eye. That kind of change and growth takes time and consistency. When that alarm clock sounds in the morning for you to get to the gym, you better have a strong reason you choose to go; otherwise, you might find yourself like so many others, pressing snooze and giving up.

What goes hand in hand with a is self-discipline. Self-discipline is a skill. Some people developed it early on in life and seem to be naturals at it. You may not be one of those people and will have to also work at increasing your self-discipline skills. Having a clear picture of why you are making a specific healthier choice will help with self-discipline. The secret to self-discipline is to ignore the thoughts in the current moment, telling you to quit and hold the feeling of the outcome you are seeking. Return to the alarm clock in the morning, and thoughts may rise to suggest you press snooze, sleep in, and start tomorrow. Self-discipline is about setting those thoughts aside and putting your focus on an end goal. In this case, it could be how good you will feel after your workout. Knowing that you had the option to quit, but choose not to, can create a feeling of empowerment in itself. It builds self-confidence. Instead of putting your focus on instant gratification – in this instance, sleeping in – you focus on the longer-term goal and how amazing that will be to accomplish. Perhaps you have heard about the importance of mindset. Do you have a growth mindset or a fixed mindset? In a fixed mindset, you tend to believe your intelligence, talents, and traits are fixed and cannot change. In a growth mindset, you understand you can change those things through effort and persistence. Self-discipline is about having a growth mindset. Remember when I said all things are possible? It just takes focus and continued action. Maybe you hate public speaking. That does not mean you could not become a fantastic public speaker. There are many stories out there about individuals who feared public speaking and faced that fear and changed. James Earl Jones is a great example. Did you know he has a stuttering problem? He stuttered as a kid and, to this day, says it has not entirely gone away, yet he is known for his voice and speaking. In general, people tend to want instant results, and when we don't get immediately satisfied, we quit. So instead, it is necessary to focus on the action.

If your goal is to love and accept all parts of yourself, that is not a muscle you will build in a week. It will take time to start to see the change, just like lifting weights. Instead of doing the action and then looking for instant results, make the act itself the focus. That means you acknowledge your long-term goal is to have a better relationship with yourself. You understand that practice makes better, so you will not allow yourself to evaluate these tools' effectiveness until you give them a good solid chance. Instead, your goal is just to do the work like lifting weights. You know if you go to the gym for one week, even though that will make changes, it won't change that you will immediately see. If you quit after one week, declaring lifting weights does not build muscle, you will not only be wrong, but you will have missed out on an experience you said you wanted. Repetition is required to see change. Most things take time to learn. You don't start playing the piano in one week then expect to play to a full audience at Carnegie Hall.

The relationship with our selves never really has an ending point, like a relationship with another person could. It can always grow deeper and more connected the more time and effort you put into it. This journey you have chosen to take does not have an endpoint, which is not a bad thing. I often remind people it is not that you never get there; it can only keep getting better. When you commit to the actions rather than looking immediately for results, you will look back at yourself and see the change after some time of continuous effort. This is something I never tire of seeing in my private practice with clients. The recurring theme is people coming in with wants and desires. Those wants and desires tend to be pretty intense, too, as most people coming into my office feel at their wit's end and want things to change *now*! As I validate this desire and sit with them in the despair of not having what they want right now, some negative energy is freed up to do the work.

What starts to happen is that the person becomes more focused on the tools and mastering them that they shift their perspective to more internal and action-focused, they forget a bit about how life is not what they want. The tools themselves provide relief and peace. The person in front of me begins to surrender to what is and shift their focus to self-acceptance. Then, my favorite part, the outside starts to reflect the inside. I hear stories of job promotions or new jobs found, new relationships, or healed past relationships. I will never tire of that individual sitting across from me with wide eyes, proclaiming, "I manifested this."

The day you realize you are not the victim of your life, you are the author, director, and hero will be a day you never forget. You will also find yourself wanting to show others, wanting them to understand that they don't have to remain in suffering and that they, too, have the power to free themselves. Yes, it takes focus and concentration to learn this and make it a new habit, and yet it is so worth it. Back to Jim Rohn, "We must all suffer from one of two pains: the pain of discipline or the pain of regret. The difference is discipline weighs ounces while regret weighs tons." To answer that burning question, I know you still likely have: *How long do I have to do this until I see results*? Allow me to be a little annoying and answer that question with a question: How long should we allow a baby to learn how to walk? The answer is: *until.* You let a baby learn to walk until they learn to walk. And you are encouraged to use these tools until you see change. There is no question of *if* these tools work because they work! It is just a matter of how long before they work. You can quit and go back to how you have always been.

That's not wrong or bad. It is familiar, and you know what it will bring you. But you picked up this book and are still reading it because you don't like what has been coming your way in that old, familiar behavior or pattern. These tools may not bring you instant happiness, but I can promise they will bring you to change. If you want new experiences, you must do new things.

Chapter Eleven

Imagine a World

One of the goals of this book is to inspire you to start envisioning what is possible. I want to get you to tap into your imagination, where all material things come from, and get excited about what you could feel and experience. Think about it. Everything you have created started in your mind first. You are an amazing organism capable of so much more than you may have ever allowed yourself even to consider. We each view and understand the world through our belief systems and perceptions. When those filters were built on hurt, pain, suffering, trauma, it causes you to be looking through dirty filters – unless you change it. I was having a conversation with a friend the other day about their frustration with another friend's behavior. My friend vented to me about how their friend was passive-aggressive at times, and they had been at the receiving end of this passive-aggressiveness several times. My friend was angry that their friend did not even acknowledge this behavior and instead even denied it and blamed others for their reactions. Let's break this down. How do you think my friend was feeling? Angry, yes, but anger is a cover emotion. Anger is useful, it can feel empowering and motivate you to step up to change and feel better, but often we need first to acknowledge all the emotions there before we can have lasting change. What might be under the anger? Hurt? Sadness? Perhaps a sense of powerlessness as my friend felt like a victim of another's pain and then was blamed for it? Very likely and an easy one to validate as well. Of course, if this were you on the receiving end, you may have felt hurt and powerless! It was a one-sided conversation, and the passive-aggressive friend was the only one in the conversation. I am willing to bet my friend also felt uncared for, maybe unloved, unimportant. Why? Because if they were loved and important, wouldn't this friend stop to listen? Wouldn't this friend say, "You feel what from my behavior?! Oh, I am so sorry! I never meant for you to feel that!" We can validate my friend some more. Remember, validation is supporting the feelings, not the thoughts. It would feel like you are being ignored and not important when someone you believe cares about you doesn't listen or accept your feelings. We have validated and integrated by sitting and listening to the emotions that are there. We allowed them to exist because they do. If this was inner child work, I would have had my friend stand up to their friend visually in order to help build a relationship with herself. But this was a current issue happening more recently, not something that had happened in the long-ago past. That doesn't mean you can't stand up for yourself. That is still an important part, but what I will focus on here is the reflection that is being given. The reflection being how my friend perceived the experience. See, it can be so difficult to step outside of ourselves to see our patterns, to see our unconscious programming, to know what we want to change or need to change to create what we desire. The universe gives us a gift and show's us our behavior outside of ourselves. When something unpleasant happens outside of you, your reaction and thoughts are a message to what is not serving you. In the Bible, it states, "Ask and you will receive, and your joy will be complete."[3] .I believe this is 100% true. But to receive, we have to make space for what we want, and when we ask, it invites the universe to help us clean house—time to stop hoarding all the garbage that is not serving you. If you want change in your life, you must accept complete responsibility for your current experience of reality in order to start that change. Notice I said *the experience of* reality. I am not blaming you for the things that have happened to you in your life. I am holding you responsible for how you perceive them, as that is what is creating your experience of reality.

Back to my friend. What do they need to take responsibility for? What is the universe showing them that they are ready to release? What is the garbage that is not serving them, taking up space for what they want instead? Let's step back into the observer and look at this situation with curiosity. Remember, you can't be traumatized and curious at the same time. What is the friend doing? They are not taking responsibility for their behavior. What is my friend doing? Believing that to be validated and feel important and loved, those around them need to hear them, validate, and see them. That is a very simplified summary of what is happening.

So let's look first at my friend's reaction. Are these beliefs serving them? Heck no! Waiting for someone outside of you to validate you is torture! Yes, it feels fantastic to be validated outside of yourself, and yes, you deserve outside validation, but do you need to wait for it to feel loved and accepted? Of course not. That is the point of this book. What can my friend do? They can begin to challenge their beliefs. Read my book, so they understand childhood wounds and subconscious patterns. They can step outside of themselves and recognize that their friend may be in a subconscious pattern that came from their childhood. It has nothing to do with my friend or how lovable or worthy they are. That does not mean my friend has to tolerate the behavior. My friend can set a boundary, but they are setting this boundary coming from a place of love rather than fight or flight. See the difference? One is empowering, and the other is a place of victimhood.

What else can my friend learn from this experience? Here is a hard one with which most people struggle. How is this person's behavior similar to something I do? Yuck, right? Your mind might yell at you, *That's not me, I don't do that! I would never!* If your mind does do this, you went into fight or flight, so take a breath and get back into the observer role. Our greatest teachers are not the individuals that make us feel good; it's the individuals that trigger us and make us want to run, blame, or fight. Why is that, you ask? Because our responses are about us. If you are having a strong reaction, there is something inside you that has been raised as a danger flag. You see something in yourself that you don't like, or this person activates your fears, and you have gone to the other extreme, which is just the other side of the same coin. Sometimes it can be both, and I will show you why.

With my friend, her pattern of becoming angry and attacking in reaction to the passive-aggressive behavior of the other friend is a direct reflection of herself. And, it is also a direct reflection for us all really because we have all been guilty at some point or another of having an unconscious behavior and blaming something outside of us for it. When you blame something outside of you for your reaction, you are giving away your power. I am not saying it is simple to master your emotions, but you are the one in charge of your emotions. You are the driver of your car, even if you don't know how to drive it. Since this was my friend, I know they have a pattern of quickly getting angry when feeling attacked. They are a deeply caring individual and work hard to be aware of how they affect others, but they have a fighting pattern when they feel unsafe. I reminded my friend of this, and their immediate response was that it was like when they were younger. We all have a choice here. Keep repeating our patterns or take responsibility, do the work, and change our relationship with ourselves.

My friend was triggered by passive-aggressive behavior. She was attempting to push away the passive-aggressive behavior. Something about that behavior felt unsafe for her. So I had her explore what about being passive-aggressive is bad. To find her underlying fear, I asked my friend what the worst-case scenario that could come from being passive-aggressive? She told me it would be pushing everyone away and being all alone. To which I replied, that is one of your fears. See, my friend worked hard not to be passive-aggressive as she had a fear that would lead her to be alone, rejected, or abandoned. Since this was fear, she was triggered when she saw the behavior in others. In my friend's case, she works hard to make sure others feel seen and heard. This is not a bad thing, but it does not feel good when it comes from a place of fear of being rejected. When that fear of rejection is triggered, my friend becomes angry and fights. There is plenty of inner child work to do here. These feelings and fears did not start with her passive-aggressive friend. Let's briefly go through the work and see how it might change my friends' world.

My friend sits with the feelings experienced had when their friend was passive-aggressive, getting familiar with them and allowing them to exist in the body, permitting them to be there. By next asking themselves when the first time is they can remember feeling this, a memory comes up, and the work with their inner child can begin. The work includes taking the memory and changing their perspective on it. The brain doesn't know the difference between fantasy and reality, with numerous studies proving this. In my opinion, my friend is going back in time and rescuing themself, providing for themselves the adult they needed but didn't get. What happened hasn't changed; it's not needed. What has changed is their perspective of what happened, providing themselves the love, support, and acceptance required. Most likely, there was another individual in the memory, and my friend stands up for her younger self through this inner child work, creating trust within themself, acknowledging their importance, and that they matter. Then syncing up their brain by bringing their younger self to the present, showing them all the wonderful things in their life. As my friend finishes up the rest of the inner child work with one memory, they can go back and work with others. This repetition creates familiarity, and they are making it more familiar with what having a loving, accepting relationship with themselves offers. Having *cleaned their house of the garbage,* the former belief systems, and perspective on the world, they have made space for the feelings they really want.

When we change how we view the world, the world changes for us. My friend feels calmer and more confident. When the passive-aggressive friend repeats their behavior, my friend is no longer triggered, instead finding calm compassion. My friend also appreciates the hurt their friend is in and has empathy and compassion for this person. The subconscious pattern of becoming angry and attacking in return has been broken. There is no need to fight because there is no threat. By breaking the unconscious pattern, they have freed up limited possibilities and are choosing new, more beneficial, and healthy possibilities from a place of calm and compassion.

What do you think life will look like for you when you make your choices from a calm and compassionate place? How will the world look when you do this? The power to change your life is truly in your hands. It all lies in the relationship with yourself.

End Notes

---

[1] Maleficent directed by Robert Stromberg (Walt Disney Pictures, 2014).

[2] Friedrich Nietzsche was a German philosopher and critic during the late 1800s. His challenge of religion, morality and philosophy affected generations of poets, psychologists, philosophers and other creative endeavors.

[3] John 16:24, New International Version

Made in United States
Troutdale, OR
03/11/2026

47600570R00062